FASTBAC

190

The Case for the Smaller School

Weldon Beckner

PHI DELTA KAPPA
EDUCATIONAL FOUNDATION

WELDON BECKNER

Weldon Beckner is currently professor and chairman of Educational Administration and Supervision, College of Education, Texas Tech University in Lubbock, Texas. Previous responsibilities at Texas Tech have included director of development and chairman of Curriculum and Instruction. Prior to joining the faculty at Texas Tech, he was a teacher and administrator in Texas and Colorado at elementary, junior high, and high school levels.

Beckner's special interest is applying theories of leadership and school change to curriculum development and teacher effectiveness. Most recently his research and publication efforts have focused on the needs and opportunities of smaller schools. With an initial grant from the Moody Foundation, he founded at Texas Tech a National Center for Smaller Schools to sponsor research and development activities relative to smaller schools. A major thrust of the Center has been application of microcomputer technology to administrative and instructional activities of smaller schools. Another project, currently in its beginning stages, will involve a selected group of smaller school districts in a university-school cooperative effort to apply research on effective schools to leadership efforts by local administrator-teacher teams.

Beckner's publications include five textbooks and numerous journal articles. He has recently completed a national study of small school needs, which will soon be published.

Series Editor, Derek L. Burleson

The Case for the Smaller School

By Weldon Beckner

Library of Congress Catalog Card Number 82-063061
ISBN 0-87367-190-2

Bloomington, Indiana

This fastback is sponsored by the Ohio State University Chapter of Phi Delta Kappa, which made a generous contribution toward publication costs.

The chapter sponsors this fastback in honor of Miss Bessie Gabbard, "first lady" of Phi Delta Kappa, generous patron of the Phi Delta Kappa Educational Foundation, and beloved member of the Ohio State University Chapter. She believed in the dream and helped it come true.

We thank you, Bessie, keeper of the dream.

Table of Contents

Introduction

New York City is building smaller schools! That recently reported fact may surprise some, but it is another indication of the reviving interest in smaller schools. Initially, New York City opted to build its new schools smaller because of a lack of sites for large buildings, but it was soon recognized that there were several other advantages for smaller schools. Thus in a sense, we have come full cycle from the day when much of the public education in this country was conducted in the one-room rural schoolhouse. But factors other than nostalgia for the one-room school are contributing to this renewed interest in smaller schools. Changing educational philosophy, new teaching strategies and instructional technology, environmental policies, land costs, and population shifts are some of the factors of modern life that lead many to think that the small school is alive and well, making its own contributions to young people and their communities.

During the years of rapid industrial growth and urbanization, school districts were consolidated and school buildings became larger. Most educators began to assume that what was right for urban/suburban education was also right for schools in small towns and rural communities. Influenced by the thinking or prominent educational leaders such as James Conant, we attempted to organize all schools on an urban model. All high schools should be "comprehensive"; all junior high and elementary schools should be large enough to benefit from mass education techniques used in the cities. Rural and small-school educators attempted to imitate their metropolitan counterparts by imposing large-school solutions on small-school problems. "Better" too often meant "like urban schools" instead of "better" in meeting the needs of children and youth in rural and other small-school settings.

As we explore in this fastback the revival of interest in smaller schools and examine their potential and their problems, keep in mind that approximately one-third of all public school students are currently enrolled in nonmetropolitan area schools. They actually outnumber those in central city schools. And the incidence of poverty and low achievement is higher in rural schools than in metropolitan schools. Yet, special funding from federal and other sources to alleviate these problems in rural schools has been less than one-third of that available to urban schools. Also keep in mind that the 1980 census showed that there has been heavy migration to the South and West and to rural areas and smaller communities, which is expected to continue throughout the 1980s. This has resulted in growth in school populations in those areas, which will require educational adaptations that build on the strengths of the existing schools as they accommodate growth and change.

The educational well-being of this large segment of our student population is important to our society. We must, therefore, give more attention to our smaller schools; and in the process, we may find that there are many proven successful practices in small schools that apply to large ones as well. Indeed, lest we forget, many of the so-called "innovations" in education have long been common in small schools (e.g., individualized instruction, cross-age grouping, and peer teaching).

The Legacy of the Small School

Former governor of Minnesota, Albert Quie, at the time a member of the National Council on Excellence in Education, recently recalled his days as a rural school boy and later as a rural school board member. He noted that one of his first goals as a young board member was to consolidate schools. He has now changed his mind, because he realizes that the traditional rural school characterizes all those qualities that make schools excellent. Quie also commented that he was particularly impressed with the number of national leaders who are products of small schools.[1] If we examine more closely some of the elements of nonurban society and education, we will find that our country cousins and small-school educators have much to offer us about how to prepare students in all schools for the uncertain future.

The traditional small school was an extension of its community. Indeed, it was difficult to determine just where education ended and community life began around the school. The school was a community responsibility; the community was a school responsibility, with the school serving as the center for secular festivities, community entertainment, and cultural enlightenment. "Community education" and "parent involvement" are not new concepts, although they may take a somewhat different look today than they did 50 or 100 years ago.

No argument is being made here for romanticizing the small school, but there does seem to be much that is valuable from the legacy of these schools. Building on that legacy, we should be able to overcome most of the shortcomings of small schools today by keeping what is best from the past and using the opportunities for improvement offered by the present. At the same time, it is quite possible that many of the problems encountered in urban and other large school settings might find solutions in small-school traditions and practices. Some of the better known educational "innovations" of today, which have roots in the small (and usually rural) schools of the past, include the following:

Nongraded classrooms
Flexible scheduling
Individualized instruction
Independent study
Peer teaching/tutoring
Team teaching
Continuous progress
Mastery learning
The school as a "family"
Student activities
Parent-teacher conferences and committees

The Question of Minimum Size

Of the various "reform" efforts in education in the last 50 years, perhaps the most successful has been the consolidation of rural and small school districts. From 1930 to 1972 the number of school districts in this country decreased from 128,000 to 16,960, and the number of one-room elementary schools from 149,000 to 1,475. At the secondary level, the number of traditional four-year high schools (the kind usually found in rural and small districts) was cut in half; at the same time the enrollment in secondary schools tripled.[2]

School consolidation efforts succeeded primarily because educators accepted without question the assumption that consolidation of small schools, with their less well trained teachers and limited financial resources, would solve most of the problems long considered endemic to rural education. Even those parents and educators with reservations about consolidation conceded that it would save money through economies of scale and increased operating efficiency. This assumption needs some scrutiny.

It is true that traditional measures of educational achievement have shown students in small and rural schools to be lagging behind their urban counterparts. However, it can be argued with considerable validity that students in these smaller schools may be learning values in self-reliance, human relations, character development, and other areas not measured by standardized tests that urban students have often been noted to lack. Although small schools can't always provide the extensive curriculum offerings found in urban schools, they do offer a solid basic education program and have far fewer problems with discipline, drugs, vandalism, and truancy.

Advocates of school consolidation have used such measures as years of school completed, extent of functional illiteracy, grade retardation, and percent of youth attending college to bolster their case. These measures seem to indicate that educational achievement in smaller rural schools falls short of that in large schools. However, these differences largely disappear when adjustments are made for the migration of many rural, well-educated young adults to metropolitan areas and for the lower socioeconomic status of the general population in rural areas. Add to this recent data from the National Assessment of Educational Progress that indicate improved performance among rural children and youth to the point of reaching national averages for some ages in science, reading, functional literacy, and social studies and it would seem that the purported advantages of consolidation have probably been exaggerated considerably. Even the argument of being able to offer the advantage of more specialized and advanced classes in larger schools is muted by the fact that only a small percentage of exceptional students actually take the specialized classes.

Questions can also be raised relative to the economic advantages of school consolidation. Granted, increased size will produce some economies, but the extent of savings depends on other factors, such as the quality of education provided and transportation costs. A recent review of research on school size economies concluded that elementary education may experience economies for relatively small populations (300 to 600 students). Secondary schools and school districts may experience economies over a greater pupil range. However, evidence from the research available indicates that application of these findings to most cost questions must be considered carefully and on a case-by-case basis, because cost factors other than size are often changed by the circumstances. Increased funding required by an expanded curriculum, additional student services, transportation, and other costly operations in bigger schools and school districts may largely offset savings related to increased size.[3]

Since there is not clear-cut evidence for the superiority of either large or small schools on the basis of cost, comprehensiveness, student development, and academic achievement, we must turn to other considerations in our quest for answers to the optimum school size question. For example, currently, when public confidence in education is dwindling, school administrators and school boards are asking how to restore citizen and parent support for schools. It is no secret that parents have long favored smaller schools, particularly if they were "neighborhood" schools. And there is little argument that parent-teacher/parent-school relationships are usually better in smaller school districts or in smaller schools in large districts.

In trying to answer the question about optimum school size, it is difficult to prove empirically the advantage of smaller schools. Rather, we must look to common sense, observation, and logical reasoning for evidence about the values of education in small schools. In the next section we shall consider both empirical and other kinds of evidence as we discuss in more detail the advantages of smaller schools.

Advantages of Smaller Schools

In discussing the advantages of smaller schools, I have grouped my arguments into six areas: 1) community relationships and control, 2) finance, 3) administration, 4) teachers, 5) students, and 6) curriculum and instruction.

Community Relationships and Control

Historically the rural school has served as a community nucleus, with strong support from parents and other community members and close working relationships between the staff and members of the community. The community's awareness of school policies and of what is going on in the school results in a kind of informal accountability. More parental involvement in school activities results in mutual expectations for student behavior. The community exerts more direct control over the school and thus sees that the school serves the specific needs of the community.

Finance

Because citizens feel a more direct relationship to the schools, they tend to be more willing to support them financially. Since school facilities are usually available for various community uses, taxpayers can avoid unnecessary duplication of public facilities. Administrators and school board members can exercise clear supervision of school expenditures.

Administration

Relationships between faculty and administrators (many of whom have some teaching responsibilities) are usually closer, and more teachers and students are likely to be involved in making administrative decisions. Administrators' relationships with students, parents, and other community members are usually more cooperative. There is less bureaucracy and red tape; there are fewer regulations. Therefore, it is easier to make changes in the organization and administration of the school. Schedules can be altered more readily to accommodate instructional objectives. Record-keeping and reporting activities are less complicated.

Teachers

Because relationships with administrators tend to be more personal, there is a greater sense of community among the staff. In a small school each teacher must assume a variety of roles, including involvement in guidance functions, thus providing a breadth of perspective to the total school program. Teachers are more likely to be respected as valuable members of the community. And since they tend to come from small communities, they are more likely to understand and to adapt to small-town community life. They know their parents better and therefore receive better cooperation in resolving problems that arise. Because teachers have to be generalists, they are more receptive to participating in team teaching, program planning, and other cooperative ventures. Teacher-student ratios are usually lower.

Students

School morale tends be higher in smaller schools. Students have more pride in their community, their school, and in themselves, which results in improved student conduct; because there is less alienation, fewer students have poor attitudes toward school. Students are more likely to approach teachers and other school personnel with individual needs and problems. Because each student is needed, a larger percentage is involved in student activity programs. Such programs are more likely to be learning experiences for many rather than a stage for a few stellar performers. Because individualization is easier to carry out, students have a greater opportunity to discover their individual identity and potential. Finally, students are the ultimate beneficiaries of the closer relationships among parents, teachers, administrators, and the community.

Curriculum and Instruction

Individualization of instruction is a necessity; therefore the school is likely to be learner-centered, with more independent study and cross-age grouping likely to occur. It is easier to make changes in curriculum organization and instructional materials and to achieve curriculum articulation and coordination. It is easier to arrange schedules and to work out other logistical problems related to instruction (field trips, assembly programs, work-study programs, etc.).

The advantages inherent in small schools are not automatic, of course. If not properly used by administrators and teachers, they could become hindrances to good education. Small class size has little advantage if teachers persist in lecturing when small-group procedures would be more appropriate. Scheduling flexibility could become scheduling inflexibility if administrators persist in using scheduling systems developed for large schools. By recognizing the values of smallness and then taking advantage of them, educators can do much to enhance the learning of students.

Disadvantages of Smaller Schools

Although the purpose of this fastback is to make a case for small schools, I would be remiss if I did not give attention to the inherent disadvantages of small schools. In many cases, disadvantages are simply the other side of the coin of the advantages. The intent in discussing the disadvantages is to identify ways to alleviate or overcome problems brought about by smallness. Such solutions will be discussed later in this fastback. As in the previous chapter, the disadvantages are grouped into the same six categories: community relationships and control, finance, administration, teachers, students, and curriculum and instruction.

Community Relationships and Control

Smaller communities tend to be more conservative and slow to meet the changing needs of students now and in the near future. If the community is isolated, as well as small, there is likely to be cultural impoverishment and parochialism. Because the school is so central to the life of the community, the community may exercise an overbearing influence on the school, particularly relative to values and customs. Most small communities are homogeneous in most respects and therefore provide less opportunity for students to have contact with those from different backgrounds and cultures. The general tendency to value the notion that "bigger is better" might affect the community self-concept. Such inferiority feelings may make it difficult to maintain high morale in the school.

Finance

Small schools are not inherently efficient financially. To provide a quality program requires a relatively high per-student expenditure. The tradition of paying for schools with local ad valorem taxes causes a wide variation in the ability of small communities to support their schools. Most small communities have only one or two major kinds of economic activity, so when economic misfortune hits one of these tax-supporting businesses, it is difficult for the rest of the community to make up for this loss of support. As state legislatures come under the control of urban constituencies, state laws relative to school finance tend to discriminate against smaller communities. Further, federal education programs have been designed primarily for urban areas, both in kind and in allocation of money. Most smaller communities tend to have an older, more conservative citizenry, who are usually less able, and less willing, to vote for taxes necessary to support quality schools.

Administration

Administrators in small schools and school districts have little, if any, assistance. Most principals have a part-time secretary at best, and few specialized services to students and teachers are available. Superintendents must complete all the reports and other chores required by state and federal agencies. Without help from intermediate or cooperative agencies, it is almost impossible for them to submit the proposals necessary to get supplementary funds. Small-school administrators are often those with the least experience and professional preparation. There is limited opportunity for professional growth of administrators, because without subordinates to assume responsibilities it is difficult for them to take time away from school. Funds for professional development are also usually very limited. The fact that many principals also teach can be a disadvantage since it takes time and drains their energy away from administrative and leadership responsibilities. Administrators are particularly susceptible to pressure from the community, because they are in daily contact with parents and community leaders. The potential benefit of close contact with teachers and students may become a disadvantage if relationships are not good.

Teachers

Attracting and keeping quality teachers is one of the greatest difficulties faced by small schools, especially in rural and economically disadvantaged areas. Lack of adequate housing is often a problem. Teachers, as well as others in small or isolated schools, often suffer from an inferiority complex about their school and their professional effectiveness. Professional development for teachers is especially difficult. Because teachers are frequently isolated from colleagues in their special field, there are limited opportunities for professional interaction. Operating as a generalist has its values, but with a limited number of teachers to cover the curriculum, it may mean that some are required to teach outside their field of professional strength. Multiple lesson preparations are usually a necessity. Three or more preparations at the secondary school level are common, and drain a teacher's time and energy. Supportive services to help teachers deal with various student problems, if available at all, are usually limited. Academic freedom is often curtailed by the conservative attitudes of the community and the school board.

Students

Students have fewer choices relative to course offerings and teacher assignments. This frequently presents difficulties when transferring to another school. Sometimes feelings of inferiority make it difficult for students to adjust to university life or to working in large cities. There are fewer provisions for students needing special education, and fewer support services are available (guidance, counseling, health, psychological, instructional). The usual homogeneity of the student body limits their exposure to varied ethnic, socioeconomic, and cultural groups of American society. A negative bias by teachers toward particular families in the community or bad experiences with older siblings may cause difficulties for students who don't really deserve them.

Curriculum and Instruction

When small schools mimic larger schools in organizing their curriculum, the result is often course offerings with limited scope and depth. Unique organizational and instructional techniques designed to accommodate smaller numbers of students and teachers in smaller schools are largely undeveloped or seldom used. New developments in teaching technology are seldom available. Lack of financial resources often limits the availability of instructional materials. There is often an overemphasis on the academic areas of the curriculum because they cost the least and because of the conservatism of the community. Special programs for exceptional students are often inadequate or nonexistent.

Meeting the Needs of Smaller Schools

The discussion to this point has dealt with the many advantages—and disadvantages—common to most small schools. Because there are too many students in these schools to neglect their educational needs, we must find ways to make the most of inherent values found in small schools and their communities. In this chapter we shall consider what is needed to improve small schools and rural education with suggestions concerning student needs, finance, community values, curriculum and instruction, personnel, and policy control.

Meeting Student Needs

Young people in small and rural schools today are not drastically different from their city cousins. This increasing homogeneity has occurred because of many factors in the modern world, most noticeably transportation and television. Furthermore, the variety of student needs is similar in urban and rural areas; there are just fewer of each variety in smaller rural schools. It might seem that it would be easier in smaller schools to give individual attention to those with special needs, but this is not necessarily so because there are fewer professional personnel to work with the wide variety of needs.

Those research studies that have made allowances for social class, economic conditions, and ethnic groupings have found that academic performance in small schools is about equal to that in metropolitan schools. This says to us that for academically inclined and motivated youngsters small schools are satisfactory. It is a different story, however, for students with special needs. A recent study of rural schools found that problems of their students are actually more severe than those of students in urban schools. Rural school students are more likely to be classified as illiterate and to score lower on national achievement tests. They enroll in school at an older age, progress through school more slowly, and complete fewer years of school. These problems are primarily concentrated in low-income areas and among minorities.

In addition to the problems of minority and poor young people in smaller rural schools are the problems of those who desire vocational education. Typically, the only vocational courses offered are agriculture and home economics; and demand for study and work in these fields is not as high as it once was. Rural youth are often interested in areas requiring special vocational training, but neither the facilities nor the teachers are available.

Perhaps the most difficult problem for smaller rural schools is providing special education to a small number of handicapped children, who may be scattered geographically. A wide range of handicapped conditions spread over multiple grade levels presents a situation few teachers can manage adequately. We have both a moral and legal obligation to meet the special needs of all handicapped children and youth, wherever they may live.

Development of social skills for coping with the modern world is often overlooked in smaller rural schools. In fact, this "invisible curriculum" may be even more important for these children and youth than the academic curriculum.

It should be clear that the wide diversity of needs common to students in both metropolitan and rural areas requires innovative and even daring efforts by educators in smaller schools and by those in the community who support their efforts. "Business as usual" is not enough for meeting the educational needs for today's technological society; this is especially true in those communities where schools are unavoidably small.

Meeting Financial Needs

Finances plague almost all school districts these days, but the situation for rural and other small schools is especially severe. Traditionally the local property tax has been the primary source of income for schools, even though most authorities on school finance agree that it produces many inequities. Some districts have a hundred times more property valuation to tax per student than do other districts in the same state. Obviously, those students who happen to live in a tax-poor district do not receive equal educational opportunities. Neither is it fair to expect property owners in poor districts to assume an excessive share of the state's responsibility for public education. Districts with a valuable property base can raise much more money with a small tax rate than poor districts can with a much higher tax rate. Because of this recognized inequity, over 50 years ago states began to amend school finance formulas in various ways to help poorer districts.

Most state school finance formulas designed to provide greater equity use a "foundation" plan based on the value of property in a district and the tax rate school boards choose to levy. If a specified minimum levy does not produce a certain minimum number of dollars for each school child, then the state contributes funds to bring the local budget up to a "foundation" level. This minimum level, unfortunately, does not usually provide enough for an adequate program. Even in these times of relatively good teacher supply, "minimum foundation" districts cannot attract the necessary numbers of good teachers for their schools. Compounding the problem is that state funds are usually not available for buildings and other capital outlay. Neither is adequate allowance made for high transportation costs necessary in sparsely populated districts. In addition, mandated programs for special education students impose financial burdens.

Achieving equity in school finance is a complicated issue, which is compounded by concerns of small school districts about local control of finances. Based on past experiences with forced school consolidation and other state regulations, small-school officials fear that increased state finance will bring with it more state control and unwanted and unnecessary rules and regulations. While there may not be a direct relationship between centralization of school finance and centralization of other educational decision making, there is enough evidence to make educators and community members wary. And the more recent federally funded educational programs are viewed with even more caution. Thus small-school officials are pulled between wanting additional sources of funding for their schools and fearing increased state and federal controls.

If state and federal contributions are to supplement local finance efforts, they should be in appropriate amounts and distributed in such a way as to achieve the goals of equity, stability, and flexibility.

Regardless of place of residence, each student should be provided an "equal opportunity" for a good education. This goal is not easily achieved. It does not mean that equal dollars will be spent per child nor that all children will receive the *same* education. Rather, consideration must be given to facts of population sparsity, socioeconomic conditions, ethnic and language background, and other variables that affect the educational needs of children and youth.

Local districts need to be able to develop their programs on the basis of a financial plan that is stable and predictable. Reasonable lead time must be provided between allocation of state and federal funds and the implementation of programs at the local level so that school officials have the assurance of some stability in planning and budgeting for needed programs and services.

The goal of flexibility will allow districts to develop educational programs best suited to local community needs and to the different characteristics of individual students. This places definite limits on the degree of state or federal control over local educational programs.

Meeting Community Needs

Small communties, particularly those in isolated settings, have a wide variety of needs that schools can properly and successfully serve. A few examples will illustrate the larger dimensions of the school's role in meeting the needs of smaller communities.

Educational needs of the community include more than what goes on in the schoolhouse. They also include self-development, basic education, cultural development, leisure time activities, recreation, vocational education, health education, etc. Serving community education needs provides close ties between the school and community.

Economic needs of the community are another category calling for the attention of educators. Many small communities today suffer from economic stagnation and decline, although there are notable exceptions. The flight of many of the younger and more capable people to urban areas has compounded traditional economic problems caused by geographic isolation, cultural homogeneity, decline of agriculture, and extreme conservatism. The schools should have a central role in helping to solve these economic problems in order to improve the overall well-being of the community.

Quality of life in a community is determined by a whole spectrum of factors, some of which relate to education and some of which don't. Values development and maintenance, interpersonal relations, religious beliefs, crime and juvenile delinquency, drug and alcohol abuse, opportunities for personal development, the performing arts, and a host of other factors determine the overall quality of life in a community and quality of life for each member of the community. The school, as an integral part of the community, can be of great help in enhancing the quality of life in a community.

Meeting Curriculum and Instruction Needs

The school curriculum must emphasize both the needs of the local community and those of the larger world affecting that local community. The curriculum must relate to the everyday lives and problems of the students, but it must also relate to the "outside" world. Throughout such a curriculum should be an emphasis on the options available to young people both within and beyond the local community.

Generally, the most pressing curriculum and instruction needs in small schools relate to scope, flexibility, organization, individualization, and teacher competence. There must be a strong foundation in basic skills and an emphasis on practical skills and learning by doing. Liberal education must be tied to vocational education, with an emphasis on individual initiative, independence, and self-direction. The ideal curriculum in small communities should encompass the concept of the school as community and the community as school.

Meeting Personnel Needs

The ample supply of teachers in most of the country during the past few years has relieved some of the severe personnel needs small schools had in the past. However, there has certainly been no surplus of *good* teachers available to small districts. Bright young teachers tend to be attracted by either higher salaries of urban areas or they want to be "where the action is." Both research and experience tell us that the teachers most likely to accept positions in smaller schools and then stay there are those who themselves grew up in small communities. Others may be attracted by what they perceive as the romanticism of rural life or by the necessity of getting a job somewhere. But few remain in the small school unless there are other more compelling reasons for their being there in the first place.

Although there has been considerable research and speculation about how to train and recruit teachers for small schools, probably the best long-range solution for meeting the personnel needs of small schools is to recruit from the supply of those who have grown up in small communities and who have had their field experience and practice teaching in a small school.

With the developing teacher shortage in fields such as mathematics, science, and education of the handicapped, small school districts face serious problems in attracting and holding good teachers in those fields. Salaries are not the whole answer, although improving them will help. Such factors as housing, the teaching environment, recreation and leisure opportunities, social life, and opportunities for personal and professional development probably have more influence than salary in recruiting and holding teachers in small communities. Doing something about these factors is even more difficult than improving salaries.

Personnel needs in small schools are not limited to classroom teachers. Just as serious is the shortage of good administrators and student service personnel or the loss of promising young school administrators to larger and more affluent districts. It is a discouraging fact that, with notable exceptions, those who continue in leadership positions in small schools tend to be either those who, because of mediocre abilities, have little opportunity to advance to a larger district or those whose avocations and "moonlighting" interests keep them in the community but at the same time take much of their time and energy.

To meet the present and future personnel needs in small school districts will require some bold and innovative actions, particularly by state departments of education. Teacher preparation programs will need to provide field experience and practice teaching in small communities. State certification standards will need to be modified to prepare "generalists" with credentials in more than one field, particularly at the secondary level. At the same time, school finance policy may need to be modified to allow extra compensation for those who are willing to serve in small schools, to provide adequate facilities, and to support a curriculum that of necessity may be more expensive per student than in a larger school district.

Meeting Control Needs

For the past half century small communities have seen control of their schools slip away. Consolidation of small school districts, formation of cooperatives and intermediate service units, increased state aid with concomitant controls, and increased federal control resulting from civil rights legislation and regulations tied to various aid programs have dispersed the traditional authority of local school officials. Whereas local school boards were once in almost total control of their schools, they now feel that they have little say concerning how their schools are conducted.

How much local control is best is an issue that is still unsettled. Local control carries with it great responsibility. Many school boards have shown that local control can also mean local neglect of schools or discrimination against certain members of the community. It is doubtful that local school boards will ever enjoy the degree of control they once knew. Nevertheless, it is generally recognized that local input and control are essential to strong community support.

If community leaders demonstrate a willingness to provide an adequate and equitable education for all young people in the community and also provide for community educational needs, they are likely to maintain a higher degree of local autonomy. However, it's a lot more work to create locally-relevant curricula, to use the community as a learning resource, to share ideas and resources among neighboring schools, and to use modern technology to provide for individual differences. It is much easier (and less expensive) to simply hire a teacher, buy standard textbooks, and put students into a classroom all day long. Local school leaders must take the initiative in meeting the unique needs of small schools if they wish to be masters of their community's educational destiny.

How Do We Get There From Here?

Recognizing the needs and the potential needs of small schools is relatively easy; meeting the needs and fulfilling the potential requires considerably more initiative, imagination, and ingenuity. Let us begin by looking at some important social indicators and trends that have implications for smaller schools as the first step in seeing how we can get there from here.

Social Indicators and Trends

More than one authority has pointed out that the changes in schools during the past 50 years have been primarily quantitative. There are fewer schools but they are larger. The school year is longer. Teachers have more training. There are more courses available to students and more instructional resources available to teachers. There are more students in school; they stay in school longer; and they represent a much wider range in ability and special needs. More of them are going to college. Qualitative changes, those actually affecting the way we do things in schools, are much less evident. In the next 50 years the need is for qualitative change in small schools as well as in their urban counterparts.

In the recent past the trend has been in the direction of specialization, centralization, and consolidation. Now, however, we are seeing countertrends that recognize the reality of smaller schools in rural communities and that question the efficacy of specialization, centralization, and consolidation.

Since 1930 the number of school districts in the United States has been reduced by almost 90%. Yet, of those remaining, more than half enroll fewer than 1,000 students; and about 20% of the nation's student population is in districts with fewer than 2,500 students.[4] With the current movement of people from large urban areas to the South and West, to rural areas, and to smaller cities, it becomes increasingly obvious that small schools cannot be ignored or left to develop in unplanned fashion.

Population movements in our country will likely result in rapid social change in many rural communities. Educators in those communities can expect increasing enrollments, new ideas, and new expectations. Other population trends that will have an impact on schools are: 1) an increasing percentage of older and middle-aged persons and a smaller percentage of children, 2) a greater number of single-parent homes and working mothers, 3) stronger competition for jobs as more women enter the work force, and 4) an increasingly strong voting block of older citizens.

It is important to recognize the demographic trends mentioned above as we think about improving small schools, but we must not lose sight of the fact that there is considerable diversity among the small and rural schools of the nation. Tom Gjelten has classified them into five groups: 1) the "stable" districts, the classic stereotype of a rural school usually found in white, middle-class farming communities; 2) the "depressed rural" districts found mostly in the South; 3) the "high-growth" communities typical of boom-town situations; 4) the "reborn" or renaissance districts enjoying a revitalization due to high in-migration rates; and 5) the truly "isolated" districts located on islands or in mountainous or desert areas.[5]

Common to these school districts are their small enrollments, but other variables unique to each type of community should keep us from making too many hasty generalizations about how to improve small schools. While each community may be homogeneous, the differences among the various small communities of the country are tremendous.

The indicators and trends relative to personnel needs, use of modern technology, finance, and control, all of which were discussed earlier, are also important—perhaps the most important indicators and trends in terms of what is actually likely to happen in small schools.

National, State, and Local Policy

Perhaps the most important issue related to small schools is the recognition that they exist, that they will continue to exist, and that they deserve their share of national and state attention when it comes to school improvement efforts. M. Ann Campbell, former Nebraska State Commissioner of Education, expressed the issue well with a story she told in a speech delivered at the National Rural Education Seminar in Washington, D.C., in 1982.[6]

> An old gardener while laying a stone wall in a country estate was asked by the owner why he used so many small stones along with the large ones. "It's like this, " he said, "these stones are like men. Many small men like me are needed to keep the big ones in place. If I leave small stones out, the big ones will not stay in place and the wall will fall."

As applied to the future of small schools, this means that the school consolidation policies of the past will be curtailed. They have no doubt served a good purpose, but there are better alternatives today. They include programs of technical assistance, special allowances for necessary transportation costs, cooperative arrangements of various kinds among small districts, special financial allowances for unavoidably small schools and school districts, and unique curriculum and instruction arrangements. More specific recommendations of this type came from the National Seminar on Rural Education in 1979 and the follow-up Regional Rural Roundtables in 1980. The recommendations were numerous and were directed more specifically to federal initiatives, but most of them are appropriate for attention at any level of government. The following selection from these recommendations indicates the more important positions taken.

1. Eliminate antirural bias.
2. Establish funding formulas and mechanisms that will provide maximum local flexibility in dealing with the needs of special rural populations.
3. Help rural districts provide equitable services to special populations by providing additional support for transportation, facilities, and delivery systems.
4. Encourage development of locally relevant curricula by providing resources for collecting data; reviewing, adapting, or generating new materials.

5. Encourage and support community-based educational organizations and initiatives, particularly those serving traditionally neglected populations.

6. Provide technical assistance to rural school districts in order that they can compete for program funds.

7. Support communication networks to encourage sharing of information about rural education by small school districts and agencies at all levels of government.

8. Combine funding from various agencies or programs in order to improve the delivery of educational services for community development.

9. Provide specialized rural preservice and inservice training programs for teachers and other educational personnel.

10. Establish incentive programs to attract personnel specially trained for smaller school districts.

11. Develop and utilize appropriate technology for both instruction and administrative services.

12. Provide guidance and counseling programs and materials that focus on the unique needs of students in these schools.

13. Provide vocational programs that develop a broad base of diversified knowledge and skills needed for employment, self-employment, or for supplementary income.

14. Reconsider the policy of school consolidation because of the rising costs of fuel for school transportation.

15. Develop energy conservation measures.[7]

Best Practices

Curriculum and Instruction. A curriculum that is appropriate for small schools will relate directly to the community and everyday lives and problems of students, without neglecting college and vocational preparation and world understanding. Experiential learning, as developed in some of the alternative and outdoor schools, is particularly appropriate for small schools. Text materials should relate to both rural and urban environments. Courses should provide a strong focus on personal/community development. To overcome the inferiority syndrome common in many small communities and schools requires strong doses of community and school pride that recognize the community heritage and its accomplishments.

Teaching methods should take advantage of the natural small-school assets of cooperation, coordination, and close student-teacher relationships. Fortunately, modern technology provides a method of individualizing instruction if we will learn how to make the best use of it. With the aid of microcomputers, every student can come closer to a private tutorial experience.

Innovative ideas (many of which have their roots in the one-room schools of the past) that are applicable to small schools include small-group instruction, individual study contracts, block scheduling arrangements, individual and small-group projects, community-based learning experiences, outdoor education, peer and cross-age tutoring, team teaching, and using community members in planning and providing learning opportunities.

Personnel. Staffing in smaller schools is one of the most difficult problems to solve. Even today with an ample supply of teachers, it is difficult to recruit good teachers who are willing to live and work in smaller or isolated communities. About 80% of the teachers currently working in small schools grew up in the country or in towns of less than 10,000 population.[8]

A study of 45 school districts in South Dakota identifies characteristics of good teachers in smaller schools.[9] They include the following:

1. Have a ranch or small town background and an appreciation of the countryside.
2. Able to work independently without supervision and maintain classroom discipline.
3. Demonstrate a positive attitude toward youth and teaching.
4. Accept the community as it is and be involved in its affairs.
5. Able to adapt to the limited resources of small schools in rural communities.

This same study emphasized the need for good inservice programs, offered on site and designed to serve the expressed needs of the teachers involved.

Here are some things administrators and school board members should keep in mind when recruiting in order to keep good teachers in smaller schools.

1. Recruit those prospects who grew up and went to school in small towns and rural areas.

2. Try to get teachers who are certified and capable of teaching in more than one subject area or grade level and who are prepared to supervise more than one kind of student activity.

3. Look for teachers who are flexible and able to adjust to the lifestyles, shopping facilities, cultural life, and recreational opportunities in small communities.

4. Recruit teachers who are able to accept being scrutinized by parents and other community members with whom they are in daily contact.

5. Try to attract teachers who have enough cultural background and knowledge of the world to help students overcome their limited perspective and experience.

6. Offer the very best salary and fringe benefit plan possible, even if it means neglecting some other budget items.

7. Arrange for good housing if it is not available, even to the extent of subsidizing it if necessary.

8. Do everything possible to help teachers with their own professional development, including good local inservice programs, financial aid for graduate study, and appropriate salary increments for professional development activities.

9. In recruiting, emphasize teacher autonomy, direct access to administration, the slower pace of living, smaller class size, community involvement, and other advantages of smaller schools.

10. Work with community leaders to provide recreational opportunities for teachers, including various kinds of trips and access to recreational facilities in the community or nearby. See that teachers are included in the recreational activities of the community.

11. Be sure that teachers know that they are the most important part of a good school and treat them like the professionals you want them to be.

Finance. Securing adequate funding is at the heart of most small-school problems, although there are some districts blessed with ample funds. Following are some things that can be done to alleviate the finance problems common to smaller schools:

1. Give attention to the special needs of rural and small schools, those associated with small size, population sparsity, isolation, and rural diversity.
2. Avoid seeking simple solutions to complex problems of small school finance.
3. Recognize that providing quality education in small communities is generally more costly than in cities.
4. Accept the fact that spending patterns, e.g., for transportation, will be different in small school districts.
5. Provide for better accessibility to special grants, programs, and subsidies from state, federal, and private sources.
6. Adopt policies so that the school and other community agencies can more easily share their resources.
7. Seek supplementary funding from state and federal sources to increase salaries and other financial benefits for teachers.
8. Urge states to assume an increased proportion of total educational costs.
9. Seek state aid formulas that will provide proportionately greater assistance to districts with low property wealth and low income.
10. Avoid tying reorganization or consolidation to financial incentives.
11. Allow budget decisions to be as decentralized as possible. This will require some flexibility in state standards.
12. Urge states to assume full costs of transportation and capital expenditures.

Organization. The essence of improving education in small schools is captured in one word—cooperation. In earlier efforts at cooperation (some would call it forced cooperation) local districts were consolidated into larger administrative units. Now, other approaches are being used. The three most common are: 1) specialized services provided through decentralized offices of the state education agency; 2) special district education service agencies, either legally constituted or cooperative; and 3) educational cooperatives. The special district education service agencies are probably providing more programs and services to local districts, but either one of the other approaches may be more appropriate for a particular state or region.

Whatever the organizational approach, there are a variety of instructional and administrative activities appropriate for cooperation. They may be as simple as two teachers from two different schools working together, or as complex as a statewide network of intermediate agencies that provide an array of special services. Some of the areas of cooperation include instructional materials centers, pupil personnel services, area vocational programs, textbook exchange programs, consultants for inservice programs and curriculum development, driver education courses, psychological and guidance services, computer services, and cooperative purchasing.[10] Other possibilities include cooperation in offering advanced courses, or those in less demand; sharing of vocational teachers or other special staff (e.g., counselors, psychologists, librarians, etc.); sharing use of microcomputer labs and simulated vocational education programs. The possibilities for cooperation are limited only by the imagination and ingenuity of educators and the willingness of administrators to establish a structure through which cooperative efforts might function.

Thus far we have considered the kinds of cooperation that are inter-school or inter-district in nature. There are even more exciting possibilities for cooperation among teachers and administrators within individual schools and school districts. Team planning and team teaching, peer observation to improve teaching, sharing of teaching materials, and scheduling arrangements whereby teachers may have the time to share ideas and to improve teaching and learning in their schools—these are some of the ways the professional staff can cooperate to improve their schools.

Other organizational plans or administrative arrangements provide the flexibility that is needed for improving teaching and learning in small schools. They include:

1. Nongraded schools (both elementary and secondary)
2. Large group, small group, independent study plans
3. Four-day school week
4. Flexible scheduling
5. Cross-age grouping
6. Correspondence courses
7. Advanced standing courses
8. Community education programs
9. Flexible compulsory attendance requirements so students can take advantage of opportunities to learn outside the school
10. Summer programs, both academic and nonacademic

Leadership. It is not the intent of this fastback to explore the process and strategies of educational leadership. However, without effective leadership, the other ideas we have considered for improving small schools are not likely to happen. So, let us consider briefly some of the aspects of leadership that are particularly applicable to improvement of education in small schools.

As mentioned earlier, citizens in rural areas and smaller communities tend to be conservative, slow to accept change, somewhat suspicious of anything coming from outside the community, and often slow to agree on anything. However, they will mobilize to improve their schools if there is an emphasis on local determination of needs and local control of program and policy changes that are suggested. They will support what they see as being directly beneficial to the community as long as it remains under local control and does not involve excessive bureaucratic entanglements.

The following guidelines, based on both theory and experience, suggest ways that leaders can bring about change to improve the educational program in small or rural schools:

1. The role of the designated school leader is to coordinate and facilitate the work of parents, teachers, students, and community

leaders. They are the ones to consult in terms of school and community needs; and they should be in control of the decision making involved in what needs to be changed.

2. Human relations and communications skills are needed by leaders directing the change process, as well as by all those involved in school improvement efforts. It may be necessary to provide such training.

3. Any suggested innovations must be directly related to agreed-on educational goals. Community values and customs are important considerations in setting educational goals. To the extent possible, leaders should strive for consensus (not compromise of majority vote) when involving the community in setting goals for school improvement.

4. Outside experts should serve as resource people only, not as designers or implementers of a new program.

5. When making innovations, it is important to build an "institutional base" to ensure that sufficient expertise and support remain in the community to carry on when outside consultants are gone. Part of this base is adequate finances to carry on the innovation and make it permanent.

Let's Get On With It!

It is my hope that school leaders who read this fastback will find ideas that will motivate them to *take action.* Reams of articles and books are written every year on the problems and needs in education, but little happens as a result. Superintendents, principals, and other school leaders need to study their local situations, consider the possibilities for improvement, and take action to maximize the strengths and minimize the weaknesses of smaller schools. In a time when our educational institutions face financial crises and retrenchment, those responsible for the operation of our schools might find it easier to stick with the status quo than to promote needed change and improvement. But we need dynamic and bold leadership to provide opportunities for students in smaller schools, and perhaps even to help show the way for larger school systems. History indicates that we can expect such leadership from small-school educators as they build on the legacy of small schools to fulfill present and future needs of students and society.

Notes

1. *Rural Education News* 33, no. 2 (Summer 1982):1-2.
2. *School Size: A Reassessment of the Small School*, Research Action Brief, Number 21, (1982).
3. William F. Fox, *Relationship Between the Size of Schools and School Districts and the Cost of Education*, (Washington, D.C.: Department of Agriculture, Technical Bulletin No. 1621, ERIC EA 012706, 1980).
4. *Digest of Educational Statistics*, (Washington, D.C.: U.S. Department of Education, 1981).
5. Tom Gjelten, *Rural Education News* 33, no. 2 (Summer 1982):2.
6. M. Anne Campbell, "Chief State School Officer Muses on Nurturing Rural Schools," *Rural Education News* 33, no. 2 (Summer 1982):6.
7. *The National Seminar on Rural Education.* (Washington, D.C.: National Institute of Education, 1979).
8. Faith Dunne and William S. Carlsen, *Small Rural Schools in the United States: A Statistical Profile*, (Washington, D.C.: The National Rural Center, 1981), pp. 10-11.
9. Thomas E. Moriarty, "Unique Qualities of Rural Teachers in Western South Dakota," *The Small School Forum* (Winter 1980-81):12-13.
10. Everett D. Edington, "The Regional Approach to Serving Rural Youth," *The Rural Educator* (Winter 1980-81):1-5.

Selected References

Burdin, Joel L., and Poliakoff, Lorraine L., eds. *In-Service Education for Rural School Personnel.* ERIC (ED 073 082), 1973.

Digest of Educational Statistics, Washington, D.C.: U.S. Department of Education, 1981.

Dunne, Faith, and Carlsen, William S. "Small Rural Schools in the United States: A Statistical Profile." Mimeographed. Washington, D.C.: The National Rural Center, 1981.

Fox, William F. *Relationships Between the Size of Schools and School Districts and the Cost of Education.* Washington, D.C.: Department of Agriculture. Technical Bulletin No. 1621, ERIC (EA 012 706), 1980.

Fratoe, Frank A. "Education Training Programs and Rural Development." Mimeographed. Washington, D.C.: U.S. Department of Agriculture, 1979.

_____ "Problems and Strengths of Rural Education." *The Rural Educator* (Fall 1980):13-23.

Gjelten, Tom. "The Rural Experience of Federal Education Aid." *The Rural Educator* (Winter 1980-81):6-15.

_____ *The Rural Experience with Federal Education Aid.* ERIC (ED L93 002), 1980.

Gjelten, Tom, and Nachtigal, Paul. "Improving Rural Education: Past Efforts, Some Ideas for the Future." ERIC (ED 172 979), 1979.

Jess, James D. "School Finance in Rural Education." *The Rural Educator* (Winter 1980-81):30-35.

Mehaffie, Shamus. *A Survey of Current and Future Educational Issues of Small West-Texas Secondary Schools.* Lubbock, Tex.: International Center for Arid and Semi-Arid Land Studies, Texas Tech University, 1973.

Moriarty, Thomas E. "Problems of Rural Superintendents in Western South Dakota." *The Rural Educator* (Fall 1981):1-5.

Nachtigal, Paul M. *Improving Rural Schools.* Washington, D.C.: National Institute of Education, 1980.

_____ "Rural Education: The Next 50 Years." *The Rural Educator* (Winter 1980-81):30-35.

Niess, Charles. "A Nongraded Program for the Small High School." *NASSP Bulletin* (February 1966):19-27.

O'Neal, Linda, and Beckner, Weldon. "Rural Education: Past and Present." *The Rural Educator* (Fall 1980):13-23.

_____ "Rural Education: Past and Present (Part II)." *The Rural Educator* (Winter 1981-82):17-27.

Rural Education News 33 (Summer 1982).

School Size: A Reassessment of the Small School. Research Action Brief, Number 21. Eugene, Ore.: ERIC Clearinghouse on Educational Management, February 1982.

Seifert, Edward H., and Simone, Penny. "Personnel Practices That Keep Rural Schools Open and Community Based." *The Small School Forum* (Winter 1980-81):12-13.

Sher, Jonathan P., ed. *Educational in Rural Armerica.* Boulder, Colo.: Westview Press, 1977.

Summary of Research on Size of Schools and School Districts. Arlington, Va.: Educational Research Service, Inc. 1974.

The National Seminar on Rural Education. Washington, D.C.: National Institute of Education, 1979.

Fastback Titles *(continued from back cover)*

107. Fostering a Pluralistic Society Through Multi-Ethnic Education
108. Education and the Brain
109. Bonding: The First Basic in Education
110. Selecting Instructional Materials
111. Teacher Improvement Through Clinical Supervision
112. Places and Spaces: Environmental Psychology in Education
113. Artists as Teachers
114. Using Role Playing in the Classroom
115. Management by Objectives in the Schools
116. Declining Enrollments: A New Dilemma for Educators
117. Teacher Centers—Where, What, Why?
118. The Case for Competency-Based Education
119. Teaching the Gifted and Talented
120. Parents Have Rights, Too!
121. Student Discipline and the Law
122. British Schools and Ours
123. Church-State Issues in Education
124. Mainstreaming: Merging Regular and Special Education
125. Early Field Experiences in Teacher Education
126. Student and Teacher Absenteeism
127. Writing Centers in the Elementary School
128. A Primer on Piaget
129. The Restoration of Standards: The Modesto Plan
130. Dealing with Stress: A Challenge for Educators
131. Futuristics and Education
132. How Parent-Teacher Conferences Build Partnerships
133. Early Childhood Education: Foundations for Lifelong Learning
134. Teaching about the Creation/Evolution Controversy
135. Performance Evaluation of Educational Personnel
136. Writing for Education Journals
137. Minimum Competency Testing
138. Legal Implications of Minimum Competency Testing
139. Energy Education: Goals and Practices
140. Education in West Germany: A Quest for Excellence
141. Magnet Schools: An Approach to Voluntary Desegregation
142. Intercultural Education
143. The Process of Grant Proposal Development
144. Citizenship and Consumer Education: Key Assumptions and Basic Competencies
145. Migrant Education: Teaching the Wandering Ones
146. Controversial Issues in Our Schools
147. Nutrition and Learning
148. Education in the USSR
149. Teaching with Newspapers: The Living Curriculum
150. Population, Education, and Children's Futures
151. Bibliotherapy: The Right Book at the Right Time
152. Educational Planning for Educational Success
153. Questions and Answers on Moral Education
154. Mastery Learning
155. The Third Wave and Education's Futures
156. Title IX: Implications for Education of Women
157. Elementary Mathematics: Priorities for the 1980s
158. Summer School: A New Look
159. Education for Cultural Pluralism: Global Roots Stew
160. Pluralism Gone Mad
161. Education Agenda for the 1980s
162. The Public Community College: The People's University
163. Technology in Education: Its Human Potential
164. Children's Books: A Legacy for the Young
165. Teacher Unions and the Power Structure
166. Progressive Education: Lessons from Three Schools
167. Basic Education: A Historical Perspective
168. Aesthetic Education and the Quality of Life
169. Teaching the Learning Disabled
170. Safety Education in the Elementary School
171. Education in Contemporary Japan
172. The School's Role in the Prevention of Child Abuse
173. Death Education: A Concern for the Living
174. Youth Participation for Early Adolescents: Learning and Serving in the Community
175. Time Management for Educators
176. Educating Verbally Gifted Youth
177. Beyond Schooling: Education in a Broader Context
178. New Audiences for Teacher Education
179. Microcomputers in the Classroom
180. Supervision Made Simple
181. Educating Older People: Another View of Mainstreaming
182. School Public Relations: Communicating to the Community
183. Economic Education Across the Curriculum
184. Using the Census as a Creative Teaching Resource
185. Collective Bargaining: An Alternative to Conventional Bargaining
186. Legal Issues in Education of the Handicapped
187. Mainstreaming in the Secondary School: The Role of the Regular Teacher
188. Tuition Tax Credits: Fact and Fiction
189. Challenging the Gifted and Talented Through Mentor-Assisted Enrichment Projects
190. The Case for the Smaller School
191. What You Should Know About Teaching and Learning Styles
192. Library Research Strategies for Educators

PDK Fastback Series Titles

1. Schools Without Property Taxes: Hope or Illusion?
3. Open Education: Promise and Problems
4. Performance Contracting: Who Profits Most?
6. How Schools Can Apply Systems Analysis
7. Busing: A Moral Issue
8. Discipline or Disaster?
9. Learning Systems for the Future
10. Who Should Go to College?
11. Alternative Schools in Action
12. What Do Students Really Want?
13. What Should the Schools Teach?
14. How to Achieve Accountability in the Public Schools
15. Needed: A New Kind of Teacher
17. Systematic Thinking about Education
18. Selecting Children's Reading
19. Sex Differences in Learning to Read
20. Is Creativity Teachable?
21. Teachers and Politics
22. The Middle School: Whence? What? Whither?
23. Publish: Don't Perish
26. The Teacher and the Drug Scene
29. Can Intelligence Be Taught?
30. How to Recognize a Good School
31. In Between: The Adolescent's Struggle for Independence
32. Effective Teaching in the Desegregated School
34. Leaders Live with Crises
35. Marshalling Community Leadership to Support the Public Schools
36. Preparing Educational Leaders: New Challenges and New Perspectives
37. General Education: The Search for a Rationale
38. The Humane Leader
39. Parliamentary Procedure: Tool of Leadership
40. Aphorisms on Education
41. Metrication, American Style
42. Optional Alternative Public Schools
43. Motivation and Learning in School
44. Informal Learning
45. Learning Without a Teacher
46. Violence in the Schools: Causes and Remedies
47. The School's Responsibility for Sex Education
48. Three Views of Competency-Based Teacher Education: I Theory
49. Three Views of Competency-Based Teacher Education: II University of Houston
50. Three Views of Competency-Based Teacher Education: III University of Nebraska
51. A University for the World: The United Nations Plan
52. Oikos, the Environment and Education
56. Equity in School Financing: Full State Funding
57. Equity in School Financing: District Power Equalizing
59. The Legal Rights of Students
60. The Word Game: Improving Communications
61. Planning the Rest of Your Life
62. The People and Their Schools: Community Participation
63. The Battle of the Books: Kanawha County
64. The Community as Textbook
65. Students Teach Students
66. The Pros and Cons of Ability Grouping
67. A Conservative Alternative School: The A+ School in Cupertino
68. How Much Are Our Young People Learning? The Story of the National Assessment
69. Diversity in Higher Education: Reform in the Colleges
70. Dramatics in the Classroom: Making Lessons Come Alive
72. Alternatives to Growth: Education for a Stable Society
73. Thomas Jefferson and the Education of a New Nation
74. Three Early Champions of Education: Benjamin Franklin, Benjamin Rush, and Noah Webster
76. The American Teacher: 1776-1976
77. The Urban School Superintendency: A Century and a Half of Change
78. Private Schools: From the Puritans to the Present
79. The People and Their Schools
80. Schools of the Past: A Treasury of Photographs
81. Sexism: New Issue in American Education
82. Computers in the Curriculum
83. The Legal Rights of Teachers
84. Learning in Two Languages

84S. Learning in Two Languages (Spanish edition)

85. Getting It All Together: Confluent Education
86. Silent Language in the Classroom
87. Multiethnic Education: Practices and Promises
88. How a School Board Operates
89. What Can We Learn from the Schools of China?
90. Education in South Africa
91. What I've Learned About Values Education
92. The Abuses of Standardized Testing
93. The Uses of Standardized Testing
94. What the People Think About Their Schools: Gallup's Findings
95. Defining the Basics of American Education
96. Some Practical Laws of Learning
97. Reading 1967-1977: A Decade of Change and Promise
98. The Future of Teacher Power in America
99. Collective Bargaining in the Public Schools
100. How to Individualize Learning
101. Winchester: A Community School for the Urbanvantaged
102. Affective Education in Philadelphia
103. Teaching with Film
104. Career Education: An Open Door Policy
105. The Good Mind
106. Law in the Curriculum

(Continued on inside back cover)

See inside back cover for prices.